BULLFROGS

DOUG WECHSLER

THE ACADEMY OF NATURAL SCIENCES

The Rosen Publishing Group's
PowerKids Press™
New York

For Cousin Will who grew up in the South where bullfrogs croak, knee-deep

About the Author
Wildlife biologist, ornithologist, and photographer Doug Wechsler has studied birds, snakes, frogs, and other wildlife around the world. Doug Wechsler works at The Academy of Natural Sciences of Philadelphia, a natural history museum. As part of his job, he travels to rain forests and remote parts of the world to take pictures of birds. He has taken part in expeditions to Ecuador, the Philippines, Borneo, Cuba, Cameroon, and many other countries.

Published in 2002 by The Rosen Publishing Group, Inc.
29 East 21st Street, New York, NY 10010

First Edition

Book Design: Michael De Guzman, Michael Donnellan, Emily Muschinske

Project Editor: Kathy Campbell

Photo Credits:All photos © Doug Wechsler

Wechsler, Doug.
  Bullfrogs / Doug Wechsler. — 1st ed.
      p. cm. — (The really wild life of frogs)
  ISBN 0–8239–5855–8 (lib. bdg.)
  1. Bullfrog—Juvenile literature. [1. Bullfrog. 2. Frogs.] I. Title.
  QL668.E27 W42 2002
  597.8'92—dc21

                                                    00-012478

Manufactured in the United States of America

CONTENTS

DOUG SAYS

BULLFROGS CAN LIVE FOR 16 YEARS OR MORE IN CAPTIVITY.

BIG BULLFROGS EVERYWHERE

Jug-o-rum jug-o-rum jug-o-rum. The deep call of the bullfrog is a familiar sound near ponds and rivers. Bullfrogs are the largest frogs in North America. They can grow to be as large as 8 inches (20 cm) long. Six inches (15 cm) is a more usual length. An adult bullfrog can weigh ½ pound (227 g) or more. Bullfrogs live in most of the eastern United States and in southeastern Canada. With the help of humans, they have spread over much of the western United States, which has caused problems for other animals. Bullfrogs are usually greenish, especially on their upper lips. Their skin, from the back to the sides, is fairly smooth. Other water frogs have a ridge where the back meets the side.

Bullfrogs spend most of the day at the edge of the water. They are always ready to jump at the first sign of danger.

BULLFROG HOMES

Big ponds, little ponds, rivers, lakes, swamps, and marshes make good homes for bullfrogs. These are good places for them to raise their tadpoles as long as the ponds do not dry up each year. Bullfrog tadpoles usually take a little more than one year to grow into frogs, so they need **permanent** waters. A bullfrog's **habitat**, or home, is a shoreline and water with plants growing in it. The water is calmer where plants grow. This keeps the frogs' eggs from floating away. Underwater plants make good hiding places for tadpoles. Young bullfrogs like to warm themselves in the sun while sitting on a lily pad. A warm bullfrog **digests** its food faster so it can grow rapidly.

Bullfrogs float among water plants. Their eyes are high above the water so that they can see enemies or food.

DOUG SAYS

A BULLFROG TERRITORY USUALLY INCLUDES 10–80 FEET (3–24 M) OF SHORELINE.

WHAT DOES A BULLFROG EAT?

What does a bullfrog eat? It eats anything it wants to. The true answer is that a bullfrog eats almost any animal smaller than it is. There are a few small creatures it will not eat, at least not more than once. Young bullfrogs learn not to eat bees that sting and **millipedes** that stink and burn the tongue.

Bullfrogs have large mouths. They have roomy stomachs. A hummingbird is only a morsel. A large bullfrog can even swallow a duckling. Insects are the most common food. Bullfrogs also eat fish, crayfish, and frogs. Even young bullfrogs make a nice meal for an adult bullfrog. Large bullfrogs eat small water snakes. Large water snakes, in turn, dine on young bullfrogs. Who says nature is not fair?

The front of this male bullfrog is nearly all mouth. A bullfrog can eat an animal almost as big as it is.

DINING ON BULLFROG

If bullfrogs could write, they could fill pages with a list of their enemies. Fish, dragonfly **larvae**, water beetles, water bugs, and many other animals eat bullfrog tadpoles. Young frogs fall **prey** to snakes, birds, and raccoons.

An old bullfrog is very wary. It is quick to escape danger. Still it must watch out for hawks, large herons, and mink. There is one other enemy we should mention.

People kill thousands of bullfrogs for food. Frogs' legs are very popular in some places. In the United States, bullfrogs' legs are thought to be the best because they are the biggest.

This adult northern water snake is a major bullfrog enemy. But bullfrogs gobble up young water snakes.

TERRITORIES

Male bullfrogs defend part of their pond or stream from other males. The low-pitched jug-o-rum call can be heard for ½ mile (0.8 km). It announces, "This is my place." The place the male defends is called his **territory**. If another male bullfrog comes into his territory, he will wrestle with him to keep him out. There may be many territories in one pond. By holding a territory, the bullfrog keeps others from eating its food. It also keeps other males from mating with the females in his territory. There may be many territories in one lake or pond. The biggest bullfrog usually gets the territory in the best part of the pond. This is the area with the most food, the best places to hide, and the best places to lay eggs.

Male bullfrogs allow female bullfrogs like this one to share their territories. Males fight to keep other males out of their territory.

BULLFROG EARS

Bullfrogs do not have outer ears that stick out like ours. Our eardrum is deep down a hole inside our head. A frog's eardrum is right on the surface where you can see it. It is a big circle behind the eye. This type of ear is called a **tympanum**. When sound moving through air hits the tympanum, it makes the tympanum shake. This moves a little bone that touches the back of the tympanum. The little bone makes waves in the liquid in the inner ear. These waves hit cells that send messages to the brain. Bullfrogs' ears are tuned in best to the sounds of other bullfrogs. They sometimes can hear their enemies. Still, they are more likely to flee when they see movement or feel the ground shake.

You can tell this is a female bullfrog by her small tympanum and the white blotches on her dark throat.

DOUG SAYS

THE TYMPANUM OF AN ADULT FEMALE BULLFROG IS THE SAME SIZE AS HER EYE. THE MALE'S TYMPANUM IS MUCH LARGER.

No American frog lays more eggs than a female bullfrog. The eggs float in a thin sheet on the surface. Each time, she lays 10,000 to 20,000 eggs. In her lifetime, one female lays about 80,000 eggs. Luckily, not all eggs **survive** to become bullfrogs. If they did, the 80,000 frogs and their children and grandchildren would cover the surface of Earth before you go to college. Many eggs are eaten by fish and insects or are destroyed by **fungus**. The tadpoles are only about ¼ inch (6 mm) long when they wriggle out of the eggs. Two years later, when they are ready to change into frogs, they are the largest North American tadpoles. They can grow up to 6 inches (15 cm) long.

Top: A bullfrog tadpole's mouth has parts for feeling, scraping, and nibbling. Bottom: A large tadpole in autumn will become a frog the next summer.

A bullfrog spends the winter **hibernating** at the bottom of a pond, lake, or stream. All winter it hardly moves. It takes all of the **oxygen** it needs through its skin. The frog leaves the muddy bottom and swims to the surface when the first warm weather brings an end to winter. It takes its first breath in months.

At this time, the bullfrog is sluggish and dark. Warmth and sunlight will perk it up and make it greener.

The bullfrog is quiet in early spring. It fattens up after a long winter fast. By late spring the males start to call. The deep jug-o-rum can be heard from a ½ (0.8 km) away.

In early spring, bullfrogs are sluggish. This one tried to hide in shallow water.

DOUG SAYS

ONE FEMALE
BULLFROG
LAID
47,840
EGGS AT ONCE.

DOUG SAYS

BULLFROG TADPOLES SOMETIMES EAT OTHER FROGS' EGGS AND TADPOLES.

MORE ABOUT FROGS' LEGS

A bullfrog's legs get it into trouble because its **muscles** are large and tasty. The big muscles also get the frog out of trouble because they are powerful. Just try to grab a bullfrog. It is likely to kick free and escape.

Of course, the power of the legs shows best when the frog jumps or swims. Bullfrogs sit quietly at the edge of the pond and take a giant leap when danger arrives. In one jump, a bullfrog can travel 5 feet (1.5 m) or more. That is 10 times its body length. When the frog hits the water, its powerful legs carry it quickly to hide in safety on the pond bottom. During heavy rains, bullfrogs might hop long distances over land to distant ponds or streams.

A girl holds a bullfrog gently around his waist. This keeps the powerful legs where they cannot kick free.

THE PROBLEM WITH BULLFROGS

Bullfrogs have been released in many places where they are not **native**. You now can find bullfrogs in California, Cuba, and even South America. In most of these places, people let them go so that they can hunt the bullfrogs for their legs. When bullfrogs live in places where they do not belong, they become a big problem for other animals. Bullfrogs have eaten other frogs that are native to that place. In California, they have eaten red-legged frogs. In Oregon, they have eaten spotted frogs. In Colorado, they have gobbled up leopard frogs. These frogs have disappeared from many places where they used to live, often because of bullfrogs. It is best not to take bullfrogs to new places.

GLOSSARY

digests (dy-JESTS) When the body breaks down food you eat to use for energy.

fungus (FUN-gis) A mushroom, mold, mildew, or related organism.

habitat (HA-bih-tat) A place that has all of the things an animal needs to live.

hibernating (HY-bur-nay-ting) Spending the winter sleeping or resting.

larvae (LAR-vee) Animals in the earliest stage in life for those animals that change form to become adults.

millipedes (MIH-leh-peedz) A long, skinny animal related to centipedes and spiders with two legs per segment.

muscles (MUH-sulz) Parts of the body underneath the skin that can be tightened or loosened to make the body move.

native (NAY-tiv) Coming from and belonging to a certain place.

oxygen (AHK-sih-jin) A gas in air that has no color, taste, or odor, and is necessary for people and animals to breathe.

permanent (PER-muh-nint) Lasting forever.

prey (PRAY) An animal that is eaten by another animal for food.

survive (sur-VYV) To stay alive.

territory (TEHR-uh-tohr-ee) Land or space protected by an animal for its use.

tympanum (TIM-puh-nem) The eardrum of an insect or frog.

INDEX

WEB SITES

To learn more about bullfrogs, check out these Web sites:
http://animaldiversity.ummz.umich.edu/accounts/rana/r._catesbeiana
http://216.219.214.109/Minnesota-Herpetology/frogs_toads/Bull_frog.html